I0448427

July 2013

MILITARY READINESS

Opportunities Exist to Improve Completeness and Usefulness of Quarterly Reports to Congress

GAO-13-678

MILITARY READINESS

Opportunities Exist to Improve Completeness and Usefulness of Quarterly Reports to Congress

GAO Highlights

Highlights of GAO-13-678, a report to congressional committees

Why GAO Did This Study

Congress and DOD need relevant, accurate, and timely readiness information to make informed decisions about the use of military forces, and related resource needs. To that end, Congress requires DOD to submit a quarterly readiness report addressing various elements related to overall readiness, personnel, training, and equipment. A committee report accompanying the National Defense Authorization Act for Fiscal Year 2013 mandated GAO report on the type of readiness information available to Congress and DOD decision makers and the reported readiness of U.S. forces. In May 2013, GAO provided a classified report on readiness trends of DOD forces. For this report, GAO evaluated (1) the extent to which DOD addressed required reporting elements in its quarterly readiness reports to Congress, and (2) what additional information, if any, could make the reports more useful. GAO analyzed various readiness reports and supporting documentation, and interviewed cognizant officials.

What GAO Recommends

GAO recommends that DOD analyze alternative sources of information that could be used to meet the required reporting elements, issue guidance on the type and amount of information to be included by each service, and incorporate contextual information to improve the clarity and usefulness of reported information. DOD generally agreed with the recommendations.

View GAO-13-678. For more information, contact Sharon Pickup at (202) 512-9619 or pickups@gao.gov.

What GAO Found

In its quarterly readiness reports that covered the period from April 2012 through March 2013, the Department of Defense (DOD) addressed most but not all required reporting elements. Section 482 of Title 10 of the U.S. Code requires DOD to report on 26 elements including readiness deficiencies, remedial actions, and data specific to the military services in the areas of personnel, training, and equipment. In analyzing DOD's reports, GAO found that DOD addressed 18 of the 26 elements, partially addressed 3 elements and did not report on 5 elements. For the elements partially addressed—personnel stability, training operations tempo, and deployed equipment—reporting was incomplete because some services reported information and others did not report. When all the services reported on an element, they at times did so inconsistently, with varying amounts and types of information. For example, the services all reported information on training commitments and deployments, but used different timeframes when providing information on planned training events in the future. The services reported differently because DOD has not provided guidance on the information to be reported. For the elements that DOD did not address, including borrowed manpower and training funding, GAO found that information may exist in the department but is not being reported to Congress. For example, the Army now requires commanders to report monthly on the readiness impacts of borrowed military manpower and DOD's budget requests include data on training funding. However, DOD has not taken steps to analyze whether this information could be used to meet the related reporting element. Without issuing guidance on the type and amount of information to be included by each service and analyzing alternative information it could provide to meet the required elements, DOD risks continuing to provide inconsistent and incomplete information to Congress.

DOD has taken steps to improve its quarterly readiness reports to Congress, but additional contextual information would provide decision makers a more complete picture of DOD's readiness. Over time, based on its own initiative and congressional requests, DOD has added information to its reports, such as on operational plan assessments. In its most recent report, DOD added narrative information detailing the impact of readiness deficiencies on overall readiness and a discussion of how the services' budgets support their long-term readiness goals. Federal internal control standards state that decision makers need complete and relevant information to manage risks, and GAO found several areas where DOD could provide Congress with more comprehensive and understandable information if it added some additional context to its reports. For example, in some instances, the services report significant amounts of quantitative data, but do not include information on benchmarks or goals that would enable the reader to determine whether the data indicate a problem or the extent of the problem. For example, the Marine Corps and Air Force report mission capable rates for their specific equipment items, but do not provide information on related goals, such as the percentage of the inventory that should be kept at various capability levels. In other instances, the services have not fully explained any connections between the voluminous data they report on the required elements and the information DOD provides in the report on unit and overall readiness ratings. Without providing additional contextual information, DOD's quarterly reports may not provide clear information necessary for congressional oversight and funding decisions.

United States Government Accountability Office

Contents

Letter		1
	Background	3
	DOD Addressed Most, but Not All, Required Elements in Its Recent Quarterly Readiness Reports to Congress	7
	DOD Has Taken Steps to Improve Quarterly Readiness Reports to Congress, but Additional Contextual Information Would Be Useful	14
	Conclusions	16
	Recommendations for Executive Action	17
	Agency Comments and Our Evaluation	17

Appendix I	Scope and Methodology	21

Appendix II	Comments from the Department of Defense	23

Appendix III	GAO Contact and Staff Acknowledgments	26

Table		
	Table 1: Section 482 Required Reporting Elements	4

Figures		
	Figure 1: Overview of Quarterly Readiness Report to Congress Inputs and Format	6
	Figure 2: Overview of the Extent to Which DOD's Four Quarterly Readiness Reports for the April 1, 2012 through March 31, 2013 Period Addressed Section 482 Reporting Elements	9

Abbreviation
DOD   Department of Defense

July 26, 2013

Congressional Committees

Congressional and Department of Defense (DOD) officials need relevant, accurate, and timely information on the readiness status of U.S. forces to help them make decisions about the deployment and use of military forces and related resource needs. As a result, the Congress has enacted laws and DOD has instituted policies that require defense organizations to collect, analyze, and report readiness information. For example, section 482 of Title 10 of the United States Code requires DOD to report quarterly to Congress on military readiness,[1] which DOD does in its Quarterly Readiness Report to Congress. DOD must report on 26 elements including each readiness problem and deficiency, key indicators and other relevant information related to these problems and deficiencies, and planned remedial actions, as well as service-specific information in the areas of personnel, training, and equipment such as historical and projected personnel trends, training operations tempo, and equipment availability.

The committee report accompanying a proposed bill for the National Defense Authorization Act for Fiscal Year 2013 mandated that GAO submit a report to the congressional defense committees on the types of readiness information available to Congress and DOD decision makers and on the reported readiness of U.S. forces.[2] In May 2013, GAO provided a classified report on the readiness trends of DOD forces to the defense committees. For this report, we evaluated (1) the extent to which DOD addressed required reporting elements in its quarterly readiness reports to Congress, and (2) what additional information, if any, could make the reports more useful.

For our first objective, we reviewed legislation governing DOD readiness reporting, including section 482 of Title 10, and interviewed DOD officials. We analyzed DOD's four most recent quarterly readiness reports, which covered the period from April 1, 2012 through March 31, 2013, and compared the reported readiness information in these reports to the Title 10 requirements to identify any trends, gaps, or reporting

---

[1]10 U.S.C. § 482.

[2]H.R. Rep. No. 112-479, at 128 (2012).

inconsistencies.[3] We also interviewed officials from the Office of the Under Secretary of Defense for Personnel and Readiness, the Joint Staff Readiness Division, and each of the military services to obtain additional information and the officials' views of our assessments, as well as obtain explanations for why certain items were not addressed or not fully addressed.

For our second objective, we reviewed the types of readiness information DOD uses internally to manage readiness contained in documents such as the Joint Force Readiness Review and various service-specific readiness products and compared their formatting and contents to the four reports identified above. We reviewed the content of these reports in the context of federal internal control standards, which state that decision makers need complete and relevant information to manage risks.[4] We interviewed officials from the Office of the Under Secretary of Defense for Personnel and Readiness, the Joint Staff Readiness Division, and each of the military services to discuss the procedures for submitting readiness information for inclusion in the quarterly readiness reports and the process for compiling the full report. We also identified adjustments DOD has made to its reports, including changes the Office of the Under Secretary of Defense for Personnel and Readiness made in preparing the January through March 2013 report, and the underlying reasons for these adjustments, as well as obtained the views of officials as to opportunities to improve the current reporting.

We conducted this performance audit from August 2012 through July 2013 in accordance with generally accepted government auditing standards. Those standards require that we plan and perform the audit to obtain sufficient, appropriate evidence to provide a reasonable basis for our findings and conclusions based on our audit objectives. We believe that the evidence obtained provides a reasonable basis for our findings and conclusions based on our audit objectives. A more detailed discussion of our scope and methodology can be found in appendix 1.

---

[3]At the time of our review, DOD had compiled the report covering January to March 2013 and expected to provide it to Congress by the end of July 2013. DOD officials stated that the content and structure of this draft report provided a valid basis for our assessment.

[4]GAO *Standards for Internal Control in the Federal Government*, GAO/AIMD-00-21.3.1 (Washington, D.C.: November 1999).

Background

Section 482 of Title 10 of the United States Code requires DOD to report quarterly to Congress on military readiness.[5] The report is due to Congress not later than 45 days after the end of each calendar-year quarter (i.e. by May 15th, August 14th, November 14th, and February 14th of each year). Congress first mandated the report in 1996 to enhance its oversight of military readiness, requiring that DOD describe each readiness problem and deficiency, the key indicators and other relevant information related to these problems and deficiencies, and planned remedial actions.[6] DOD submitted its first quarterly report in May 1996. Since that time, Congress has added additional reporting requirements. Specifically, in 1997, the initial reporting requirement was expanded to require DOD to include additional reporting elements in the quarterly reports.[7] Examples of these additional reporting elements include historical and projected personnel trends, training operations tempo, and equipment availability. In 2008, an additional reporting element was added to require the inclusion of an assessment of the readiness of the National Guard.[8] For a listing of the 26 reporting elements currently required by section 482, see table 1.

[5]10 U.S.C. § 482.

[6]Pub. L. No. 104-106, § 361 (1996).

[7]Pub. L. No. 105-85, § 322 (1997).

[8]Pub. L. No. 110-181, § 351 (2008).

Table 1: Section 482 Required Reporting Elements

Each readiness problem and deficiency identified using internal DOD assessments
Planned remedial actions to address readiness problems and deficiencies
Key indicators and other relevant information related to each identified problem and deficiency
Readiness of the National Guard to support the National Response Plan in support of civil authorities
Personnel status, including the extent to which personnel are in positions outside of their specialty and/or above their grade
Historical data and projected trends in personnel strength and status
Recruit quality
Borrowed manpower[a]
Personnel stability
Personnel morale
Recruiting status
Training unit readiness and proficiency
Training operations tempo
Training funding
Training commitments and deployments
Deployed equipment
Equipment availability
Equipment that is not mission capable
Age of equipment
Condition of nonpacing items[b]
Maintenance backlog
Availability of ordnance and spares
Status of prepositioned equipment[c]
Overall readiness rating for units rated C-3 or below for the quarter and each month of the quarter by unit designation and level of organization
Resource areas that adversely affected the readiness rating for units rated C-3 or below
Reasons why the unit received a readiness rating of C-3 or below

Source: 10 U.S.C. § 482.

[a] While personnel can, at times, be temporarily diverted from the normal duties of their assigned positions, DOD does not have a common definition of borrowed manpower.

[b] According to DOD officials, there is no joint definition of nonpacing item. The Army defines pacing items as major weapon systems, aircraft, and other equipment items that are central to the organization's ability to perform its core functions/designed capabilities.

[c] DOD positions materiel and equipment at strategic locations around the world to enable it to field combat-ready forces in days rather than the weeks it would take if equipment had to be moved from the United States to the location of a military conflict.

Since DOD provided its first quarterly readiness report in May 1996, DOD and the services have invested significant resources in upgrading the systems they use to collect and report readiness information. As a result, the Office of the Secretary of Defense, the Joint Staff, the combatant commands, and the services have added numerous new readiness reporting capabilities such as the capacity to assess the ability of U.S. forces to meet mission requirements in specific operational plans. In addition, the services have also refined their respective service-specific metrics to enhance their ability to measure the readiness of their forces.

The Quarterly Readiness Report to Congress is a classified report that includes a summary of the contents of the report and multiple classified annexes that provide the required information. The report is typically hundreds of pages long. For example, the July through September 2012 Quarterly Readiness Report to Congress totaled 443 pages and the January through March 2013 report is 497 pages long. The Office of the Under Secretary of Defense for Personnel and Readiness assembles and produces the quarterly report to Congress. To do so, it compiles information from multiple DOD organizations, including the Joint Staff and military services, and its own information such as a summary of overall readiness status and prepares a draft report. It then sends the draft report to DOD components to review it for accuracy, and coordinates any comments. Once finalized, Office of the Under Secretary of Defense for Personnel and Readiness officials provide the report to the congressional defense committees (see figure 1).

Figure 1: Overview of Quarterly Readiness Report to Congress Inputs and Format

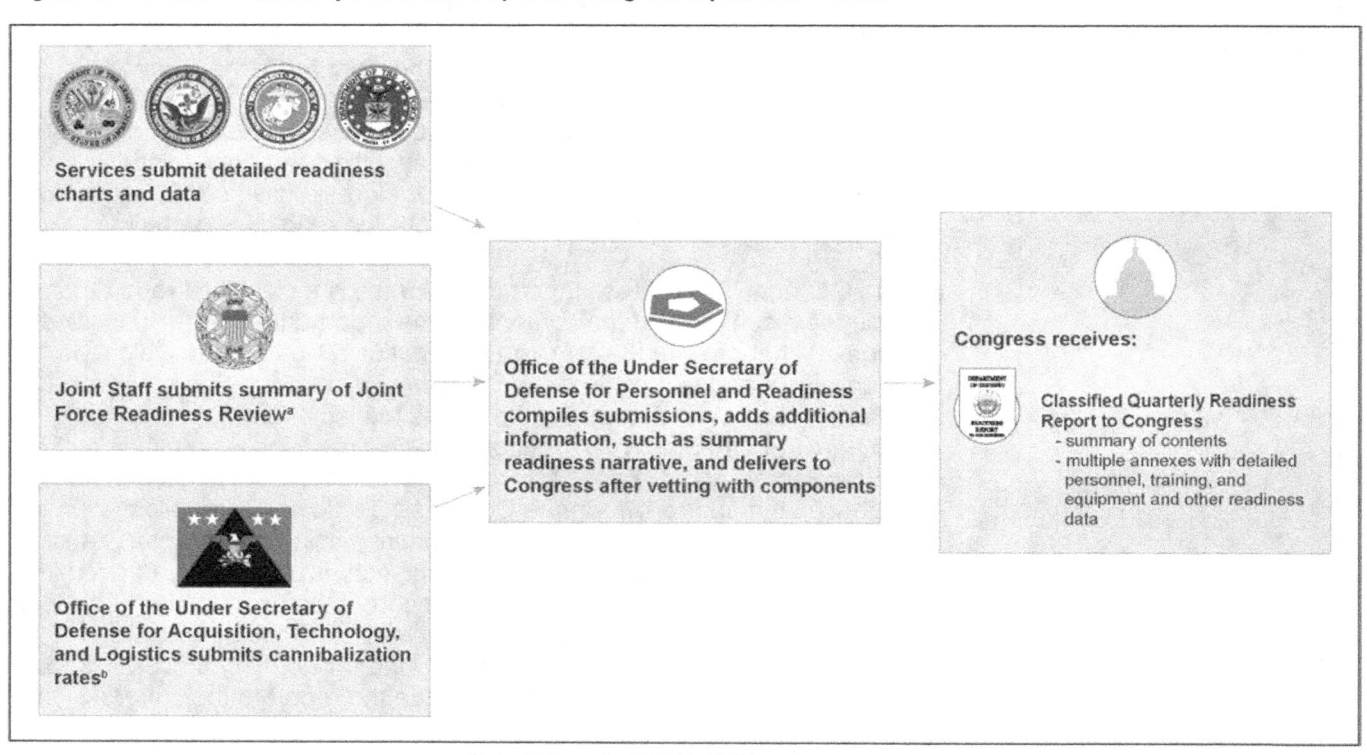

[a] Section 117 of Title 10 of the United States Code requires that the Chairman of the Joint Chiefs of Staff conduct a quarterly joint readiness review to assess the capability of the armed forces to execute their wartime missions based upon their posture at the time the review is conducted. This review is prepared by the Joint Staff.

[b] Cannibalization is defined as removing serviceable parts from one piece of equipment and installing them in another.

We have previously examined the extent to which DOD's quarterly readiness reports met section 482 reporting elements, and found that DOD's reports lacked detail, or in some cases, information required by law. For example:

- In 1998, we reported that DOD's quarterly readiness reports did not discuss the precise nature of identified readiness deficiencies, and information on planned remedial actions could be more complete and detailed to include specifics on timelines and funding requirements.[9]

- In 2003, we reported that DOD's quarterly reports still contained broad statements of readiness issues and remedial actions, which were not supported by detailed examples. We also identified gaps in the extent to which DOD addressed the required reporting elements. For example, DOD was not reporting on borrowed manpower, personnel morale, and training funding.[10]

In both reports, we recommended actions DOD could take to improve its readiness reporting. Since our 2003 review, DOD has made adjustments and expanded its readiness reporting to Congress in some areas.

DOD Addressed Most, but Not All, Required Elements in Its Recent Quarterly Readiness Reports to Congress

In its quarterly readiness reports that covered the period from April 2012 through March 2013, DOD addressed most of the 26 reporting elements required by section 482 but partially addressed some elements and did not address some other elements. We found that, for the areas that were addressed or partially addressed, the services submitted different amounts and types of information because the Office of the Secretary of Defense has not provided guidance on the information to be included in the quarterly reports. Further, we found that information may exist in the department on some of the reporting elements DOD did not address, but that DOD has not analyzed alternative information that it could provide to meet the required reporting elements.

DOD Addressed Most but Not All Required Reporting Elements in Its Readiness Reports for the April 2012 through March 2013 Period

DOD's four quarterly readiness reports that cover the period from April 1, 2012 through March 31, 2013 mostly addressed the 26 required reporting elements. In analyzing the three reports that covered the period from April 1 through December 31, 2012, we found that DOD addressed 17 elements, partially addressed 3 elements, and did not address 6 elements. In the January 1 through March 31, 2013 report, DOD's reporting remained the same except that it addressed an additional element that had not previously been addressed. As a result, our analysis

---

[9]GAO, *Military Readiness: Reports to Congress Provide Few Details on Deficiencies and Solutions*, GAO/NSIAD-98-68 (Washington, D.C.: Mar. 30, 1998).

[10]GAO, *Military Readiness: New Reporting System is Intended to Address Long-Standing Problems, but Better Planning is Needed*, GAO-03-456 (Washington, D.C.: Mar. 28, 2003).

for this report showed it addressed 18 elements, partially addressed 3 elements and did not address 5 elements. Figure 2 summarizes our assessment of the extent to which DOD's quarterly reports addressed the section 482 reporting elements.

	DOD-wide			
	Each readiness problem and deficiency identified using internal DOD assessments	●		
	Planned remedial actions	◐		
	Key indicators and other relevant information related to each identified problem and deficiency	●		
	Readiness of the National Guard to support the National Response Plan in support of civil authorities	●		

	Service specific	Army	Air Force	Marine Corps	Navy
Personnel	Extent that personnel are in positions outside of their specialty and/or above their grade	○	○	○	○
	Historical data and projected trends in personnel strength and status	●	●	●	●
	Recruit quality	●	●	●	●
	Borrowed manpower	○	○	○	○
	Personnel stability	○	●	●	●
	Personnel morale	○	○	○	○
	Recruiting status	●	●	●	●
Training	Training unit readiness and proficiency	●	●	●	●
	Training operations tempo	○	○	●	●
	Training funding	○	○	○	○
	Training commitments and deployments	●	●	●	●
Logistics	Deployed equipment	○	○	○	●
	Equipment availability	●	●	●	●
	Equipment that is not mission capable	●	●	●	●
	Age of equipment	●	●	●	●
	Condition of nonpacing items	○	○	○	○
	Maintenance backlog	●	●	●	●
	Availability of ordnance and spares	●	●	●	●
	Status of prepositioned equipment	●	●	●	●
Units below C-3[a]	Overall readiness rating for the unit for the quarter and each month of the quarter	●	●	●	●
	Resource areas that adversely affected the unit's readiness rating	●	●	●	●
	Reasons why the unit received a readiness rating of C-3 or below	●	●	●	●

● Addressed
◐ Addressed in the January through March 2013 report but not addressed in earlier reports
○ Not addressed

Source: GAO analysis of DOD data and 10 U.S.C § 482

[a] Units report an overall readiness category level (C-level) that reflects their current status of resources (personnel and equipment) and training versus requirements for wartime missions the units are designed to perform. A unit reporting C-3 possesses the required resources and is trained to undertake many, but not all, portions of the wartime mission(s) for which it is organized or designed and would require significant compensation for deficiencies. A unit reporting C-4 requires additional resources or training to undertake its wartime mission(s), but it may be directed to undertake portions of its wartime mission(s) with resources on hand.

We assessed elements as being addressed when the information provided in the report was relevant to the reporting elements set out in section 482. For example, for training unit readiness and proficiency, each of the services provided their current and historical training readiness ratings. Similarly, for recruit quality, each of the services provided high school graduation rates of recruits.

In Addressing Some Reporting Elements, DOD Reported Incomplete or Inconsistent Information

For some of the elements, DOD reported information that was incomplete or inconsistent across the services. Specifically, as shown below, for the three required reporting elements that DOD partially addressed, the information was incomplete, with only some services providing information on personnel stability, training operations tempo, and deployed equipment:

- Personnel stability: The Air Force, Marine Corps, and Navy provided information on retention rates, but the Army did not provide any information on this element.

- Training operations tempo: The Marine Corps and Navy provided information on the pace of training operations, but the Army and Air Force did not provide any information on this element.

- Deployed equipment: The Navy provided information on the number of ships deployed, but the other three services did not provide any information on this element.

Further, in instances when the services reported information on a required element, they sometimes did so inconsistently, with varying amounts and types of information. For example:

- The Air Force and Marine Corps both reported information on the age of certain equipment items, but they did not report the same amount and type of information. The Air Force reported the average age of equipment by broad types of aircraft (e.g., fighters, bombers), while the Marine Corps reported average age of specific aircraft (e.g., F/A-18, MV-22), as well as the age of its oldest equipment on hand, expected service life, and any impact of recapitalization initiatives on extending the expected service life of the equipment.

- The services all reported information on training commitments and deployments, but did not report the same amounts and types of information. First, the services used different timeframes when providing information on training commitments and deployments. The

Army provided planned training events for fiscal years 2012 through 2018, the Air Force and Marine Corps provided planned training events for fiscal years 2012 through 2014, and the Navy did not provide any information on planned training events in the future. Second, the Air Force and the Navy provided information on the number of training events executed over the past two years, while the Army and Marine Corps did not.

We found that the services have submitted different amounts and types of information to meet reporting elements because the Office of the Secretary of Defense has not provided guidance on the information to be included in the quarterly reports. Service officials told us they have received informal feedback from the Office of the Secretary of Defense regarding the data and charts they submit for inclusion in the quarterly readiness reports. For example, they have received informal suggestions for changes to how the readiness information is presented. However, service officials explained that they have not received clear guidance or instructions on the type and amount of information to present. As a result, the services have used their own judgment on the scope and content of readiness information they provide to meet the required reporting elements.

Because the services report different types and amounts of information and DOD has not clarified what information should be reported to best address the required elements, the users of the report may not be getting a complete or consistent picture of the key indicators that relate to certain elements.

DOD Did Not Report on Some Elements, Although Relevant Information May Be Available

For its three quarterly readiness reports that covered the period from April 1 through December 31, 2012, DOD did not provide any information on 6 of the 26 required elements, although in its January through March 2013 report DOD did provide information on 1 previously unaddressed element, specifically planned remedial actions. The required elements that remain unaddressed are personnel serving outside their specialty or grade, personnel morale, training funding, borrowed manpower, and the condition of nonpacing items. We found instances where information may exist within the department for some of these elements DOD did not report on. For example:

- Extent to which personnel are serving in positions outside their specialty or grade: The Navy internally reports fit and fill rates, which compare personnel available by pay grade and Navy skill code against the positions that need to be filled. Such information could potentially provide insight into the extent to which the Navy fills positions using personnel outside of their specialty or grade.

- Personnel morale: We found multiple data sources that provide information related to this required reporting element. For example, DOD's Defense Manpower Data Center conducts a series of Web-based surveys called Status of Forces surveys, which include measures of job satisfaction, retention decision factors, and perceived readiness. Also, DOD's Morale, Welfare, and Recreation Customer Satisfaction Surveys regularly provide information on retention decision indicators. Finally, the Office of Personnel Management conducts a regular survey on federal employees' perceptions of their agencies called the Federal Employee Viewpoint Survey; the results of this survey are summarized in an Office of Personnel Management report, and provide insights into overall job satisfaction and morale at the department level.

- Training funding: DOD's fiscal year 2014 budget request contained various types of information on training funding. For example, the request includes funding for recruit training, specialized skills training, and training support in the Marine Corps and similar information for the other services.

- Borrowed manpower: We found that the Army now requires commanders to report on the readiness impacts of borrowed military manpower in internal monthly readiness reports. Specifically, on a quarterly basis, beginning no later than June 15, 2013, senior leaders will brief the Secretary of the Army on borrowed manpower with a focus on training and readiness impacts.[11]

For the condition of nonpacing items element, officials from the Office of the Under Secretary of Defense for Personnel and Readiness noted that there is not a joint definition of nonpacing items across the services. The Army defines pacing items as major weapon systems, aircraft, and other equipment items that are central to the organization's ability to perform its core functions/designed capabilities, but service officials reported that they do not collect any information related to nonpacing items.

---

[11]Secretary of the Army, *Memorandum on Special Duty (Borrowed Military Manpower and Troop Diversion), Temporary Suspension of Certain Army Policy Constraints and Temporary Delegation of Certain Exception and Other Approval Authorities.* Mar. 11, 2013.

As noted previously, section 482 requires that DOD address all 26 reporting elements in its quarterly readiness reports to Congress. When asked why DOD did not provide information on certain required reporting elements, officials from the Office of the Under Secretary of Defense for Personnel and Readiness cited an analysis included in the implementation plan for its readiness report to Congress in 1998. This analysis concluded that DOD could not provide the required data at that time because, among other reasons, they lacked the metrics to capture the required data.[12] In the 1998 implementation plan, DOD noted that addressing the section 482 reporting elements was an iterative process, recognizing that the type and quality of readiness information was likely to evolve over time as improvements to DOD's readiness reporting and assessment systems came to fruition. DOD stated that it intended to continue to review and update or modify the readiness information as necessary to improve the report's utility in displaying readiness. However, since it issued its initial implementation plan, DOD has not analyzed alternative information, such as Navy fit and fill rates or satisfaction survey results, which it could provide to meet the required reporting elements. DOD officials told us they intend to review the required reporting elements to determine the extent to which they can address some of the elements that they have consistently not reported on and, if they still cannot address the elements, to possibly request congressional modifications on the required content of the reports. However, they said that they had not yet begun or set a specific timetable for this review. Without analyzing alternative information it could provide to meet the required reporting elements, DOD risks continuing to provide incomplete information to Congress, which could hamper its oversight of DOD readiness.

---

[12]Department of Defense, *Expanded Quarterly Readiness Report to Congress Implementation Plan.* Feb. 17, 1998.

DOD Has Taken Steps to Improve Quarterly Readiness Reports to Congress, but Additional Contextual Information Would Be Useful

DOD has taken steps to improve the information in its Quarterly Readiness Reports to Congress over time. However, we found several areas where additional contextual information, such as benchmarks or goals, and clear linkages between reported information and readiness ratings, would provide decision makers a more complete picture of DOD's readiness.

DOD Has Taken Steps to Add Information to Its Quarterly Readiness Reports to Congress

Over time, based on its own initiative and specific congressional requests for information, DOD has added information to its reports. For example, in 2001, it added data on cannibalizations—specifically the rates at which the services are removing serviceable parts from one piece of equipment and installing them in another. This information was added in response to a requirement in the 2001 National Defense Authorization Act that the readiness reporting system measure "cannibalization of parts, supplies, and equipment."[13] In 2006, DOD added capability-based assessment data from the Defense Readiness Reporting System and detailed information on operational plan assessments. Operational plan assessments gauge combatant commands' ability to successfully execute key plans and provide insight into the impact of sourcing and logistics shortfalls and readiness deficiencies on military risk. In 2009, it added brigade and regimental combat team deployment information.

In compiling its January through March 2013 Quarterly Readiness Report to Congress, DOD made several structural changes to expand its reporting on overall readiness. Specifically, the Office of the Secretary of Defense added narrative information and other sections, and made more explicit linkages between resource needs and readiness deficiencies in order to convey a clearer picture of the department's readiness status and concerns. In that report, DOD added:

- Narrative information detailing the impact of readiness deficiencies on overall readiness.

---

[13]Pub. L. 106-398, § 1 [Div. A. Title III, § 371], 2000 (codified at 10 U.S.C. § 117(c)).

- Discussions of how the military services' fiscal year 2014 budgets support their long-term readiness goals.

- Examples of remedial actions to improve service readiness.

- A section highlighting significant changes from the previous quarter.

Office of the Secretary of Defense officials told us that they plan to sustain these changes in future quarterly readiness reports to Congress.

Additional Contextual Information in the Quarterly Reports Would Be Useful

We found several areas where adding contextual information to the quarterly readiness reports, such as benchmarks or goals, and clearer linkages between reported information and readiness ratings, would provide Congress with a more comprehensive and understandable report. Federal internal control standards state that decision makers need complete and relevant information to manage risks.[14] This includes providing pertinent information that is identified and distributed in an understandable form.

In some instances, the services report significant amounts of quantitative data, but do not always include information on benchmarks or goals that would enable the reader to distinguish between acceptable and unacceptable levels in the data reported. For example, when responding to the required reporting element on equipment that is not mission capable:

- The Marine Corps and Air Force report mission capable rates for all of their equipment, but do not provide information on related goals, such as the percentage of each item's inventory that should be kept at various mission capability levels.

- The Navy reports on the number of ships that are operating with a mechanical or systems failure. While the Navy explains that this may or may not impact the mission capability of the vessel, it does not provide what it considers an acceptable benchmark for the number of ships that operate with these failures or the number of failures on each ship.

---

[14]GAO Standards for Internal Control in the Federal Government, GAO/AIMD-00-21.3.1 (Washington, D.C.: November 1999).

In the absence of benchmarks or goals, the reader cannot assess the significance of any reported information because it is not clear whether the data indicate a problem or the extent of the problem.

In other instances, the services have not fully explained the voluminous data presented on the required reporting elements or set the context for how it may or may not be connected to the information DOD provides in the report on unit equipment, training, and personnel readiness ratings and overall readiness. For example:

- The services provide detailed mission capable rate charts and supporting data for dozens of aircraft, ground equipment, and other weapons systems. For example, for the January through March 2013 readiness report, the services collectively provided 130 pages of charts, data, and other information on their mission capable equipment rates; this accounted for over 25 percent of the entire quarterly report. However, the services do not explain the extent to which these mission capable rates are, or are not, linked to equipment readiness ratings or overall readiness that is also presented in the quarterly reports.

- In the area of training, the Navy provides data showing the number of training exercises completed over the past two years, but does not provide any explanation regarding how this information affects training readiness ratings that are also presented in the quarterly reports.

- In the area of logistics, although the Army and the Air Force provide depot maintenance backlogs, they do not explain the effect the backlogs have on unit readiness that is also discussed in the report. Specifically, those services do not explain whether units' readiness is affected or could be affected in the future because maintenance was not accomplished when needed.

Without providing additional contextual information, such as benchmarks and clearer linkages, it is unclear how, if at all, the various data on the required elements affected unit and overall readiness.

Conclusions

To oversee DOD's efforts to maintain a trained and ready force, and make decisions about related resource needs, congressional decision makers need relevant, accurate, and timely readiness information on the status of the military forces. DOD continues to address many of the required reporting elements in its quarterly readiness reports to Congress and has periodically revised the content of the information it presents, which is an important step to making the reports more useful. However, as reflected in its more recent reports for 2012 and 2013, DOD has not always reported or fully reported on some elements, and sometimes presents detailed readiness data without sufficient context on how this information relates to or affects the information it provides on overall readiness or readiness in specific resource areas, such as equipment, personnel, and training. Without further analyzing whether information is available within the department to address the elements that it is not currently addressing, DOD cannot be sure that it has the information it needs to enhance the quality of its reporting or present options to the Congress for adjusting reporting requirements. Furthermore, unless DOD provides guidance to the services on the amount and types of information to be included in the quarterly reports, including requirements to provide contextual information such as criteria or benchmarks for distinguishing between acceptable and unacceptable levels in the data reported, DOD is likely to continue to be limited in its ability to provide Congress with complete, consistent, and useful information.

Recommendations for Executive Action

To improve the information available to Congress in its quarterly readiness reports, we recommend that the Secretary of Defense direct the Office of the Under Secretary of Defense for Personnel and Readiness to take the following three actions:

- Analyze alternative sources of information within DOD that it could provide to meet required reporting elements that DOD has not addressed in past reports;

- Issue guidance to the services on the type and amount of information to be included in their submissions for the quarterly readiness report; and

- Incorporate contextual information in the quarterly readiness reports such as clear linkages between reported information on the required elements and readiness ratings, and benchmarks for assessing provided data to enable the reader to distinguish between acceptable and unacceptable levels in the data reported.

Agency Comments and Our Evaluation

In written comments on a draft of this report, DOD concurred with two recommendations and partially concurred with one recommendation. DOD's comments are reprinted in their entirety in appendix II. DOD provided technical comments during the course of the engagement, and these were incorporated as appropriate.

In its overall comments, DOD noted that the goal of DOD is to provide the most accurate and factual representation of readiness to Congress through its quarterly reports and their ability to accomplish this relies upon our recommendations, which should facilitate improvements. DOD stated that our recommendations will be incorporated in the ongoing process of producing the quarterly readiness reports and will hopefully improve the ability to interpret the product while assisting the services in relaying their readiness concerns.

DOD also provided detailed comments on each of our recommendations. DOD partially concurred with our recommendation that the Secretary of Defense direct the Office of the Under Secretary of Defense for Personnel and Readiness to analyze alternative sources of information within DOD that it could provide to meet required reporting elements that DOD has not addressed in past reports. DOD stated the iterative process that is used to improve quarterly readiness reports to Congress will continue to seek alternative sources of information that could provide a more holistic picture of readiness across the force and that improvements in reporting capabilities and adjustments to reported readiness information should be available to provide all of the information required by section 482 of Title 10. DOD noted that it provides information on one required element, training funding, within its annual budget requests. DOD stated it will investigate ways to incorporate surrogate methods of reporting in future reports.

DOD concurred with our recommendation that the Secretary of Defense direct the Office of the Under Secretary of Defense for Personnel and Readiness to issue guidance to the services on the type and amount of information to be included in their submissions for the quarterly readiness report. DOD stated that it will continue to issue guidance to the individual services regarding types and amounts of information that may improve the readiness analysis and advance the comparative nature of separate services. DOD stated that the individual services may use distinct measures to determine specific levels of their readiness and the ability to compare these measures may not be possible or occur quarterly. Where feasible, DoD stated it will continue to attempt to align information and improve the clarity of readiness throughout the department.

DOD concurred with our recommendation that the Secretary of Defense direct the Office of the Under Secretary of Defense for Personnel and Readiness to incorporate contextual information in the quarterly readiness reports such as clear linkages between reported information on the required elements and readiness ratings, and benchmarks for assessing provided data to enable the reader to distinguish between acceptable and unacceptable levels in the data reported. DOD stated that a concerted effort is made to continuously improve the quality of analysis as well as assist with the explanation of linkages between raw data and readiness. DOD stated that this effort is tempered with the need to reduce the volume of information and provide sound examination of the effects of this data on the force. DOD noted a succinct version of readiness is provided in the executive summary included in recent reports. DOD also noted that a longer narrative supplement will continue to be provided in an attempt to enhance the clarity of the linkages and judgment of acceptability regarding the reported readiness across the force.

We are sending copies of this report to the Secretary of Defense, the Under Secretary of Defense for Personnel and Readiness, the Secretary of the Air Force, the Secretary of the Army, the Secretary of the Navy, the Commandant of the Marine Corps, and appropriate congressional committees. In addition, the report is available at no charge on the GAO website at http://www.gao.gov. If you or your staff have any questions about this report, please contact me at (202) 512-9619 or pickups@gao.gov. Contact points for our Offices of Congressional Relations and Public Affairs may be found on the last page of this report. Key contributors to this report are listed in appendix III.

Sharon L. Pickup
Director
Defense Capabilities and Management

List of Committees

The Honorable Carl Levin
Chairman
The Honorable James Inhofe
Ranking Member
Committee on Armed Services
United States Senate

The Honorable Dick Durbin
Chairman
The Honorable Thad Cochran
Ranking Member
Subcommittee on Defense
Committee on Appropriations
United States Senate

The Honorable Howard P. "Buck" McKeon
Chairman
The Honorable Adam Smith
Ranking Member
Committee on Armed Services
House of Representatives

The Honorable C.W. "Bill" Young
Chairman
The Honorable Pete Visclosky
Ranking Member
Subcommittee on Defense
Committee on Appropriations
House of Representatives

Appendix I: Scope and Methodology

To determine the extent to which the Department of Defense (DOD) addressed required reporting elements in its quarterly readiness reports to Congress, we reviewed legislation governing DOD readiness reporting, including provisions in Title 10, and interviewed DOD officials. We analyzed the four most recent Quarterly Readiness Reports to Congress that covered the period from April 1, 2012 through March 31, 2013 and compared the reported readiness information in these reports to the Title 10 requirements to identify any trends, gaps, or reporting inconsistencies.[1] Specifically, we developed an evaluation tool based on Title 10 section 482 reporting requirements to assess the extent to which the April through June 2012, July through September 2012, October through December 2012, and January through March 2013 Quarterly Readiness Reports to Congress addressed these elements. Using scorecard methodologies, two GAO analysts independently evaluated the quarterly readiness reports against the elements specified in section 482. The analysts rated compliance for each element as "addressed" or "not addressed." After the two analysts completed their independent analyses, they compared the two sets of observations and discussed and reconciled any differences. We also interviewed officials from the Office of the Under Secretary of Defense for Personnel and Readiness, the Joint Staff Readiness Division, and each of the military services and obtained additional information and the officials' views of our assessments, as well as explanations of why certain items were not addressed or not fully addressed.

To determine what additional information, if any, could make the reports more useful, we reviewed the types of readiness information DOD uses internally to manage readiness contained in documents such as the Joint Force Readiness Review and various service-specific readiness products, and compared their formatting and contents to the four reports identified above. We reviewed the content of these reports in the context of federal internal control standards, which state that decision makers need complete and relevant information to manage risks.[2] This includes pertinent information that is identified and distributed in an understandable form. We interviewed officials from the Office of the

---

[1] At the time of our review, DOD had compiled the report covering January to March 2013 and expected to provide it to Congress by the end of July 2013. DOD officials stated that the content and structure of this draft report provided a valid basis for our assessment.

[2] GAO *Standards for Internal Control in the Federal Government*, GAO/AIMD-00-21.3.1 (Washington, D.C.: November 1999).

Under Secretary of Defense for Personnel and Readiness, the Joint Staff Readiness Division, and each of the military services and discussed the procedures for compiling and submitting readiness information for inclusion in the quarterly readiness reports, changes in the reports over time, and the Office of the Secretary of Defense's process for compiling the full report. We also identified adjustments DOD has made to its reports, including changes the Office of the Under Secretary of Defense for Personnel and Readiness made in preparing the January through March 2013 report, and the underlying reasons for these adjustments, as well as obtained the views of officials as to opportunities to improve the current reporting.

We conducted this performance audit from August 2012 through July 2013 in accordance with generally accepted government auditing standards. Those standards require that we plan and perform the audit to obtain sufficient, appropriate evidence to provide a reasonable basis for our findings and conclusions based on our audit objectives. We believe that the evidence obtained provides a reasonable basis for our findings and conclusions based on our audit objectives.

Appendix II: Comments from the Department of Defense

OFFICE OF THE ASSISTANT SECRETARY OF DEFENSE
4000 DEFENSE PENTAGON
WASHINGTON, D.C. 20301-4000

JUL 16

READINESS AND FORCE
MANAGEMENT

Ms. Sharon L. Pickup
Director, Defense Capabilities and Management
U.S. Government Accountability Office
441 G Street, NW
Washington, D.C. 22548

Dear Ms. Pickup:

This is the Department of Defense (DoD) response to the GAO Draft Report, GAO-13-678, 'MILITARY READINESS: Opportunities Exist to Improve Completeness and Usefulness of Quarterly Reports to Congress,' dated June 19, 2013 (GAO Code 351821).

Thank you for the opportunity to comment on the draft report. It is the goal of DoD to provide the most accurate and factual representation of readiness to Congress through its quarterly reports. The ability to accomplish this relies upon these GAO recommendations which should facilitate improvements. The recommendations will be incorporated in the ongoing process of producing these reports and will hopefully improve the ability to interpret the product while assisting the Services in relaying their readiness concerns.

Enclosed is the Department's position on GAO recommendations. If questions should arise, please have your action officers contact Lt Col Gregory Keeton at (703) 693-0006.

Sincerely,

Laura J. Junor
Deputy Assistant Secretary of Defense
Readiness

Attachment:
As stated

GAO DRAFT REPORT DATED JUNE 19, 2013
GAO-13-678 (GAO CODE 351821)

"MILITARY READINESS: OPPORTUNITIES EXIST TO
IMPROVE COMPLETENESS AND USEFULNESS OF
QUARTERLY REPORTS TO CONGRESS"

DEPARTMENT OF DEFENSE COMMENTS
TO THE GAO RECOMMENDATIONS

RECOMMENDATION 1: To improve the information available to Congress in its
quarterly readiness reports, GAO recommends that the Secretary of Defense direct the
Office of the Under Secretary of Defense for Personnel and Readiness to take the
following action:
Analyze alternative sources of information within DoD that it could provide to meet
required reporting elements that DoD has not addressed in past reports.

DoD RESPONSE: Partially concur. The iterative process that is used to improve
quarterly readiness reports to Congress will continue to seek alternative sources of
information that could provide a more holistic picture of readiness across the force.
Improvements in reporting capabilities and adjustments to reported readiness information
should be available to provide all of the information required by section 482 of Title 10.
However, the Training Funding reporting element is included in the annual Presidential
Budget. DoD will investigate ways to incorporate surrogate methods of reporting in
future reports.

RECOMMENDATION 2: To improve the information available to Congress in its
quarterly readiness reports, GAO recommends that the Secretary of Defense direct the
Office of the Under Secretary of Defense for Personnel and Readiness to take the
following action:
Issue guidance to the services on the type and amount of information to be included in
their submissions for the quarterly readiness report.

DoD RESPONSE: Concur. DoD will continue to issue guidance to the individual
services regarding types and amounts of information that may improve the readiness
analysis and advance the comparative nature of separate services. The individual services
may use distinct measures to determine specific levels of their readiness and the ability to
compare these measures may not be possible or occur quarterly. Where feasible, DoD
will continue to attempt to align information and improve the clarity of readiness
throughout the department.

RECOMMENDATION 3: To improve the information available to Congress in its
quarterly readiness reports, GAO recommends that the Secretary of Defense direct the

2

Office of the Under Secretary of Defense for Personnel and Readiness to take the
following action:
Incorporate contextual information in the quarterly readiness reports such as clear
linkages between reported information on the required elements and readiness ratings,
and benchmarks for assessing provided data to enable the reader to distinguish between
acceptable and unacceptable levels in the data reported.

DoD RESPONSE: Concur. A concerted effort is made to continuously improve the
quality of analysis as well as assist with the explanation of linkages between raw data and
readiness. This is tempered with the need to reduce the volume of information and
provide sound examination of the effects of this data on the force. By providing an
executive summary in recent reports, a succinct version of readiness is provided. A
longer, narrative supplement will continue to be provided in an attempt to enhance the
clarity of the linkages and judgment of acceptability regarding the reported readiness
across the force.

Appendix III: GAO Contact and Staff Acknowledgments

GAO Contact	Sharon Pickup, (202) 512-9619 or pickups@gao.gov
Staff Acknowledgments	In addition to the contact named above, Michael Ferren, Assistant Director; Richard Burkard; Randy Neice; Amie Steele; Shana Wallace; Chris Watson; and Erik Wilkins-McKee made key contributions to this report.

GAO's Mission	The Government Accountability Office, the audit, evaluation, and investigative arm of Congress, exists to support Congress in meeting its constitutional responsibilities and to help improve the performance and accountability of the federal government for the American people. GAO examines the use of public funds; evaluates federal programs and policies; and provides analyses, recommendations, and other assistance to help Congress make informed oversight, policy, and funding decisions. GAO's commitment to good government is reflected in its core values of accountability, integrity, and reliability.
Obtaining Copies of GAO Reports and Testimony	The fastest and easiest way to obtain copies of GAO documents at no cost is through GAO's website (http://www.gao.gov). Each weekday afternoon, GAO posts on its website newly released reports, testimony, and correspondence. To have GAO e-mail you a list of newly posted products, go to http://www.gao.gov and select "E-mail Updates."
Order by Phone	The price of each GAO publication reflects GAO's actual cost of production and distribution and depends on the number of pages in the publication and whether the publication is printed in color or black and white. Pricing and ordering information is posted on GAO's website, http://www.gao.gov/ordering.htm. Place orders by calling (202) 512-6000, toll free (866) 801-7077, or TDD (202) 512-2537. Orders may be paid for using American Express, Discover Card, MasterCard, Visa, check, or money order. Call for additional information.
Connect with GAO	Connect with GAO on Facebook, Flickr, Twitter, and YouTube. Subscribe to our RSS Feeds or E-mail Updates. Listen to our Podcasts. Visit GAO on the web at www.gao.gov.
To Report Fraud, Waste, and Abuse in Federal Programs	Contact: Website: http://www.gao.gov/fraudnet/fraudnet.htm E-mail: fraudnet@gao.gov Automated answering system: (800) 424-5454 or (202) 512-7470
Congressional Relations	Katherine Siggerud, Managing Director, siggerudk@gao.gov, (202) 512-4400, U.S. Government Accountability Office, 441 G Street NW, Room 7125, Washington, DC 20548
Public Affairs	Chuck Young, Managing Director, youngc1@gao.gov, (202) 512-4800 U.S. Government Accountability Office, 441 G Street NW, Room 7149 Washington, DC 20548